A Christmas of Heavenly Peace

More Books in This Series

Advent Through the Eyes of Mary
Journey to Bethlehem
The Angels Speak
The Greatest of these is Love
Baubles and Bulbs, Glitter and Lights
Leave the Empty Boxes Behind
Christmas Blessings

A Christmas of Heavenly Peace

Devotions
for all the days of
Advent

Lynne Modranski

Mansion Hill Press

A Christmas of Heavenly Peace
© 2013, 2021 Lynne Modranski
All Rights Reserved

Published by Mansion Hill Press
Steubenville OH
www.MansionHillPress.com

All rights reserved. This book contains material protected under International and Federal Copyright Laws and Treaties. Any unauthorized reprint or use of this material is prohibited. No part of this book may be reproduced or transmitted in any form or by any means, electronic or mechanical, including photocopying, recording, or by any information storage and retrieval system, without express written permission from the author.

Paperback ISBN: 9781519211996

All Scripture quotations, unless otherwise indicated, are taken from the Holy Bible, New International Version®, NIV®. Copyright © 1973, 1978, 1984 by Biblica, Inc.TM Used by permission of Zondervan. All rights reserved worldwide.

CONTENTS

INTRODUCTION	7
WHAT IS ADVENT?	9
THE FIRST WEEK OF ADVENT	11
THE CANDLE OF PROMISE	
THE SECOND WEEK OF ADVENT	27
THE CANDLE OF BLESSING	
THE THIRD WEEK OF ADVENT	43
THE CANDLE OF SALVATION	
THE FOURTH WEEK OF ADVENT	59
THE CANDLE OF TRANQUILITY	
MORE BY LYNNE MODRANSKI	74
ABOUT THE AUTHOR	75

Introduction

Peace—everyone wants it. I have good news! God wants to give us peace. In fact, He sent Jesus expressly for that purpose.

Unfortunately, the commercialization of the holiday has made it anything but a peaceful season. Parties, shopping, and financial stress top the list of peace killers.

Regardless of the version you choose, scripture includes the word peace about 150 times. Prophets warn that peace can be lost, and those same men speak peace as a blessing over God's people. We're reminded of the peace God gave in the past as well as the promise He's given for peace in the present and the future.

Only one thing can give us the peace we long for this season: turning our focus toward Christ. These short readings are designed to do just that. If we continually look toward Christ instead of the trappings of the world, we will find peace—not as the world gives, maybe not even a kind we're looking for. But those who find fulfillment and contentment in the Baby in the manger instead of the list we make to celebrate His birth will find His beautiful and indescribable peace.

What is Advent?

Advent begins four Sundays before Christmas. In addition to a period of preparation, this season can be a time of anticipation.

Advent is an old Latin word that roughly translates "to come." During advent we prepare to celebrate the coming of the promised Baby and look forward to a time when the Messiah, who promised to come again, makes good His word, and rescues us from this world.

While not necessary, many light candles with the readings as a reminder that the Light of the world is coming. Some place the candles in an Advent Wreath, a circle of greenery meant to remind us of Christ's unending love as well as the eternal life He promised.

Four candles, one for each week of advent, sit around the outside. These can be any color; however, most often folks use purple, royal blue, or deep red, to symbolize the royalty of Jesus.

A white candle, the Christ Candle, placed in the middle, stands ready to light on Christmas Eve. Its color reminds us Jesus was and is perfect. His sacrifice is all that's needed to give us the gift of eternal life.

The First Week of Advent

The Candle of Promise

*If you're lighting candles,
this week you'll light one each night.*

The First Sunday in Advent
The Candle of Promise

The people walking in darkness
have seen a great light;
on those living in the land of deep darkness
a light has dawned.

. . .

For to us a child is born,
to us a son is given,
and the government will be on his shoulders.
And he will be called
Wonderful Counselor, Mighty God,
Everlasting Father, Prince of Peace.
Of the greatness of his government and peace
there will be no end.
He will reign on David's throne
and over his kingdom,
establishing and upholding it
with justice and righteousness
from that time on and forever.
The zeal of the Lord Almighty
will accomplish this.
Isaiah 9:2, 6-7

The Promised Prince of Peace

God began promising His people a deliverer as far back as the Garden of Eden, and throughout scripture the One to come was to be a bearer of peace. These few verses from Isaiah have been quoted in songs and repeated in poetry. The amazing promise they hold makes them one of the most popular prophecies.

A Child was promised, a Child who would bring light, justice, righteousness, and most importantly, peace. This Child would be a ruler, a descendant of King David, and His Kingdom would be a dynasty of serenity.

We read Isaiah's prophecy every advent because the Child has come. They called Him Jesus. He grew, and He lived. He died for His subjects, but death couldn't defeat Him. And for those who choose to serve His Kingdom, He offers life everlasting because He is the Prince, the Prince who brings peace.

The First Monday in Advent
The Candle of Promise

"To me this is like the days of Noah,
when I swore that the waters of Noah
would never again cover the earth.
So now I have sworn not to be angry with you,
never to rebuke you again.
Though the mountains be shaken
and the hills be removed,
yet my unfailing love for you will not be shaken
nor my covenant of peace be removed,"
says the Lord, who has compassion on you.
"Afflicted city, lashed by storms and not comforted,
I will rebuild you with stones of turquoise,
your foundations with lapis lazuli.
I will make your battlements of rubies,
your gates of sparkling jewels,
and all your walls of precious stones.
All your children will be taught by the Lord,
and great will be their peace.
Isaiah 54:9-13

A Promise of Unfailing Love & Peace

Depending on how you count them, you'll find 3,000 - 5,000 promises in scripture. Imagine the comfort God's chosen found in this prophecy from Isaiah when the king of Babylon ripped the nation from their homes. But what if I told you this was meant to be just as great a promise to us?

At times even the most devoted Christian feels like a city that's been "lashed by storms." Life shakes us, and we worry God might be tired of us. On those days, these verses can become a precious Christmas present, a gift from God to His people.

As the people of God, we can take courage and find hope in the fact God promised He wouldn't be angry with us. He will never take away His promise of peace. We may walk away from it, but our Maker will never remove it from us. In fact, if we allow ourselves to be taught by the Lord, our peace will be great. Christ came to rebuild us, to make us beautiful, and help us become all God originally created us to be.

This Christmas take hold of this promise. Even when you feel shaken, removed, afflicted, and uncomfortable, you are loved with an unfailing love, and God's promise of peace can never be removed!

The First Tuesday in Advent
The Candle of Promise

"My covenant was with him [Levi],
a covenant of life and peace,
and I gave them to him; this called for reverence
and he revered me and stood in awe of my name.
True instruction was in his mouth
and nothing false was found on his lips.
He walked with me in peace and uprightness,
and turned many from sin.
Malachi 2:5-6

A Promise of Life and Peace

The people of Malachi's day looked a lot like people of today. God had promised a Messiah would come, but because He took longer than they thought He should, many turned away from God, even priests, the ones who had been promised life and peace if they faithfully shared God's truth and served Him.

In 1 Peter, the apostle says we are all priests. If you have invited the Baby in the manger to be your Savior, God calls you His priest. We have been given the promise of Levi, a covenant of life and peace.

Advent is the perfect opportunity to make sure our lives revere God. As we consider the gifts we'll give this year, let's examine the present we give Christ, the gift of respect and reverence. Do we worship and live our lives in a manner worthy of the One born to be our Sacrifice?

Just as in Malachi's time, it's easy to think God is slow or has forgotten His promise to send a Messiah. Many have become lazy in their worship of our Creator, and some have completely abandoned the covenant. These folks have given up waiting and forfeited the promise of life and peace.

But some have chosen to be priests of the covenant. They share the message of a Baby born to be King, the Infant who lived to die. And for each who stands in awe of the name of Jesus, the Son who died in my Place, the promise of Malachi stands. Praise God today for His covenant of life and the promise that we may walk with Him in peace.

The First Wednesday in Advent
The Candle of Promise

"But you, Bethlehem Ephrathah,
though you are small among the clans of Judah,
out of you will come for me one who will be ruler over Israel,
whose origins are from of old, from ancient times."
Therefore Israel will be abandoned
until the time when she who is in labor bears a son,
and the rest of his brothers return to join the Israelites.
He will stand and shepherd his flock
in the strength of the Lord,
in the majesty of the name of the Lord his God.
And they will live securely, for then his greatness
will reach to the ends of the earth.
And he will be our peace
when the Assyrians invade our land
and march through our fortresses.
We will raise against them seven shepherds,
even eight commanders,
who will rule the land of Assyria with the sword,
the land of Nimrod with drawn sword.
He will deliver us from the Assyrians
when they invade our land

and march across our borders.
Micah 5:2-6

God Promised: He Will Be Our Peace

Like the scripture from Sunday, we read these verses from Micah nearly every Advent because they foretell the birth of our Savior. When the Magi came to Herod in search of the new King, Micah's words told the king's advisors where to find the Christ Child. Those learned men knew this prophecy was a promise of the One who would come from heaven to save Israel. They had no idea He would end up saving the world.

Generally, we focus on the fact the Father promised to make famous the small village of Bethlehem. God told this obscure town they would receive fame because of the Messiah's birth, but that's only part of the promise.

Verse five tells us, "He will be Our Peace." When our enemies invade, when they march through and attempt to steal God's blessings, we will have peace, because the One born in Bethlehem will be just that.

More than six hundred years before His Son came, the Creator of the Universe promised to bless the City of Bethlehem. He said an infant, older than the nation of Israel, would be born there. This Child would be a Shepherd, caring and watching out for His people, granting security and, best of all, peace.

The First Thursday in Advent
The Candle of Promise

Rejoice greatly, Daughter Zion!
Shout, Daughter Jerusalem!
See, your king comes to you,
righteous and victorious,
lowly and riding on a donkey,
on a colt, the foal of a donkey.
I will take away the chariots from Ephraim
and the warhorses from Jerusalem,
and the battle bow will be broken.
He will proclaim peace to the nations.
His rule will extend from sea to sea
and from the River to the ends of the earth.
As for you, because of the blood of my covenant with you,
I will free your prisoners from the waterless pit.
Return to your fortress, you prisoners of hope;
even now I announce that
I will restore twice as much to you.
Zechariah 9:9-12

Promise of Peace to all the Nations

From His birth to His death and resurrection, the prophets foretold every significant event in Christ's life.

Though usually reserved for the Easter season, these words from Zechariah paint a picture too big to confine to Palm Sunday. They also prophecy a King coming to us in peace.

In ancient times, a victorious king arriving on a donkey sent a message of peace and goodwill for that city. But God promised more. This Ruler would proclaim peace to the nations, to the ends of the earth. From sea to sea, any place that welcomes His rule, can experience peace and restoration. Because of the promise He fulfilled with His blood, we have freedom and hope!

During the Christmas season, we focus on the birth of a Baby, but it's the perfect opportunity to remember that this Baby grew to be King, a King who would die on a cross, whose blood would create a covenant of freedom and hope, a King who offers a promise of peace to anyone who chooses to believe.

The First Friday in Advent
The Candle of Promise

"Arise, shine, for your light has come,
and the glory of the Lord rises upon you.
See, darkness covers the earth
and thick darkness is over the peoples,
but the Lord rises upon you and his glory appears over you.
Nations will come to your light,
and kings to the brightness of your dawn.

. . .

"Then you will know that I, the LORD, am your Savior,
your Redeemer, the Mighty One of Jacob.

. . .

I will make peace your governor and well-being your ruler.
No longer will violence be heard in your land,
nor ruin or destruction within your borders,
but you will call your walls Salvation and your gates Praise.
The sun will no more be your light by day,
nor will the brightness of the moon shine on you,
for the Lord will be your everlasting light,
and your God will be your glory.

. . .

the Lord will be your everlasting light,
and your days of sorrow will end.

Isaiah 60:1-3 & 17b-21

Promise of Peace & Well-Being

I love the lights of the Christmas season. I hang them all over my house; and no matter how old I get, I still enjoy driving around to see the outdoor displays.

Hundreds of years before Jesus said, "I am the light of the world; whoever follows me will never walk in darkness," Isaiah prophesied, "Arise, shine, your light has come."

Even in Isaiah's day, this world was a dark place. But the prophet knew One born to be the Light would rise on the scene to lift humanity out of the darkness. God promised He would be a Savior and Redeemer, taking the lesser things in our life and replacing them with blessings we cannot measure. The Light came to make peace our governor. He came to show us the brightness of His dawn.

In this hectic season, it might seem as though everything but peace governs; however, when we allow Jesus to be who He came to be, our Everlasting Light, we find that well-being is indeed our ruler.

Though much of this passage will find its ultimate fulfillment in Christ's second advent, these words still hold a promise for us today. The Son came into this world to be the Light in our darkest days, glory in the midst of hatred, and the One who will turn destruction into salvation. The Baby from the manger is the Messiah, born to take our sorrow and make peace and well-being the ruler of our lives.

The First Saturday in Advent
The Candle of Promise

Your eyes will see the king in his beauty
and view a land that stretches afar.

. . .

Look on Zion, the city of our festivals;
your eyes will see Jerusalem,
a peaceful abode, a tent that will not be moved;
its stakes will never be pulled up,
nor any of its ropes broken.
There the Lord will be our Mighty One.
It will be like a place of broad rivers and streams.
No galley with oars will ride them,
no mighty ship will sail them.
For the Lord is our judge, the Lord is our lawgiver,
the Lord is our king; it is he who will save us.
Isaiah 33:17 & 20-22

A Promise of Peace to Come

During advent, we commemorate the coming of the Savior. The world celebrates a Baby who arrived two thousand years ago, and followers of Christ rejoice because we trust His promise to come again in the future.

The Bible tells us that when Jesus returns there will be a new Jerusalem. Revelation describes it as a place with no tears, no death, and no pain—a place where everything is restored.

Isaiah celebrated this same advent we wait for. He prophesied that Jerusalem will one day be a home full of tranquility. Zion (another name for Jerusalem) will be a peace-filled place, a city for all God's people. Unlike the Jerusalem of today, future Zion will be immovable and unshakable. Christ will be the King of this great city, and we will find the ultimate fulfillment of our Salvation!

As we close this first week of advent, celebrate the promises we've read this week. Rejoice in the peace we experience here on earth because Christ is the Prince of Peace, the One who rode into Jerusalem as a Peaceful King. Send up praise to the One who fulfills God's covenant of life and peace to His people. Shout out loud because the Light of the world will usher in a government of peace, and one day those who've chosen to be called by His Name will be made new along with the city whose name literally means to see peace.

The Second Week of Advent

The Candle of Blessing

*If you're lighting candles,
this week you'll light two each evening.*

The Second Sunday of Advent
The Candle of Blessing

You will keep in perfect peace
those whose minds are steadfast,
because they trust in you.
Isaiah 26:3

Those Who Trust are Blessed with Peace

All over the world people search for peace. They look for it in books, governments, music, and special days. Sometimes we even find it when we're the first out of bed on Saturday morning or in quiet moments like the one you might be having right now. However, there is only one way to find real, everlasting peace.

Isaiah spoke God's word for most of his life, and these verses reveal the heart of the Creator. He wants to grant perfect peace to anyone who stays focused on the only One who can give true tranquility.

That's why Jesus came to earth. The Father sent Him to the manger to bring peace. Each time we begin to feel tension or frustration, we need to set our mind on Christ. As we truly trust in this One whose birth we are about to celebrate, we can be blessed with the perfect peace Isaiah promised. This season set your mind on Christ and enjoy His blessing of peace.

The Second Monday of Advent
The Candle of Blessing

*"I will not accuse them forever,
nor will I always be angry,
for then they would faint away because of me—
the very people I have created.
I was enraged by their sinful greed;
I punished them, and hid my face in anger,
yet they kept on in their willful ways.
I have seen their ways, but I will heal them;
I will guide them and restore comfort to Israel's mourners,
creating praise on their lips.
Peace, peace, to those far and near,"
says the Lord.
"And I will heal them."
Isaiah 57:16-19*

God Gives the Blessing of Peace

Even those who don't walk with God understand the concept that the Creator has standards. Fewer realize our Creator does not want to be upset with us—our sin breaks God's heart. As Isaiah tells us, our Lord plans to forgive, restore, and heal.

December turns our thoughts toward presents, decorations, and carols, but advent is meant to be a time of preparation, a season to get ready to receive gifts we don't deserve. Isaiah advises that guidance and comfort will be gifted to the mourners—not a trait we usually put on our Christmas to-do list.

But this kind of mourning doesn't mean crying all the time; instead, God wants us to recognize the sin that keeps us from becoming all Christ created us to be. In fact, the prophet tells us despite our disappointing actions God sees—the greed that deserves his anger—he wants mourners to become people of praise. Even though He sees our sin, He still wants to forgive, restore, and heal.

The first weeks of advent create the perfect time to examine our lives and make sure nothing in them causes God to hide His face. Fortunately, He promises peace to those who recognize and mourn their sin. In other words, when we repent—turn away from— of whatever keeps us from our Creator, whether we are near to Him or far away, the One who sent Christ as a Baby in a manger will send the blessing of peace.

The Second Tuesday of Advent
The Candle of Blessing

*How beautiful on the mountains
are the feet of those who bring good news,
who proclaim peace,
who bring good tidings,
who proclaim salvation,
who say to Zion,
"Your God reigns!"
Isaiah 52:7*

Those Who Share the Blessing of Peace

Every time I read this verse, I ask myself, "Do I have beautiful feet?" As followers of the Infant born in Bethlehem, it's our privilege to tell the world that the Baby whose birth we celebrate died on a cross to give us everlasting life. And to have truly beautiful feet, we need to share the secret to living in the blessing of God's peace every day here on earth.

The more we understand God's love for us and let the good news soak in, the easier it is to accept the gift of salvation found only in Jesus Christ. And the more we allow God to reign in our life, the more we will experience the blessing of peace God wants to pour out on us.

You'll know you're growing when you start to share your tremendous blessing of peace with others. That's when we're able to give Jesus the very best birthday gift, because He loves it when we have beautiful feet.

The Second Wednesday of Advent
The Candle of Blessing

"For my thoughts are not your thoughts,
neither are your ways my ways,"
declares the Lord.
"As the heavens are higher than the earth,
so are my ways higher than your ways
and my thoughts than your thoughts.
As the rain and the snow come down from heaven,
and do not return to it without watering the earth
and making it bud and flourish,
so that it yields seed for the sower and bread for the eater,
so is my word that goes out from my mouth:
It will not return to me empty,
but will accomplish what I desire
and achieve the purpose for which I sent it.
You will go out in joy and be led forth in peace;
the mountains and hills will burst into song before you,
and all the trees of the field will clap their hands.
Instead of the thornbush will grow the juniper,
and instead of briers the myrtle will grow.
This will be for the Lord's renown,
for an everlasting sign,
that will endure forever."

Isaiah 55:8-13

The Blessing of Being Led in Peace

God's ways are higher than ours; His thoughts are bigger, His Word more powerful. One version says God's words make happen whatever He wants to happen. As surely as rain makes flowers grow, God's word sets God's will in motion. And the beauty of this promise is that when we allow God's word to move in our lives, we receive joy, and He gives us His blessing of Peace.

What if God's gift to you this Christmas is this blessing of Peace? What if even when it feels like nothing is going right and your problems are piling up like mountains, you could still go out with joy and occasionally have those mountains turn into songs of praise? The Creator can take the things in our life that seem like thorn bushes, brier patches, and weeds and turn them into beautiful shade trees, reminders of the depth and height of God's ways and God's will.

In order to receive the blessing of going out in joy and being led in peace, we have to be willing to be led. When we begin to believe in the power of God's word, it doesn't matter that we may never understand the depth of God's thoughts and the height of His ways. When we follow Him with joy and let Him lead, He will give us the blessing of His peace.

The Second Thursday of Advent
The Candle of Blessing

The Lord gives strength to his people;
the Lord blesses his people with peace.
Psalm 29:11

Blessing of Peace for God's People

The Lord gives strength to His people, He blesses His people with peace. Everyone wants strength and peace. Unfortunately, even folks who've read this Psalm, still strive to get strength and peace on their own.

Yet, in all the scripture I've read, I've never found a verse that tells us to work for these things. Even the verses we've shared this month remind us God gives peace.

Just like each of those beautiful packages you'll find under your tree by December 24, peace is a gift, a blessing God wants to pour out. The disappointment occurs when we attempt to get the gift for ourselves instead of putting ourselves in a place to receive God's gift.

The Psalmist makes it pretty clear—God gives strength and sends blessings of peace; however, the gift and the blessing are for God's people.

Our challenge these last few weeks of the year is to make sure we are truly God's people. We are preparing to celebrate the One who came to bring peace, but do we really belong to that One or are we just playing the game?

God wants to give us His gift of strength and His blessing of peace. Will you give Him the gift of being His people?

The Second Friday of Advent
The Candle of Blessing

The Lord's justice will dwell in the desert,
his righteousness live in the fertile field.
The fruit of that righteousness will be peace;
its effect will be quietness and confidence forever.
My people will live in peaceful dwelling places,
in secure homes,
in undisturbed places of rest.
Though hail flattens the forest
and the city is leveled completely,
how blessed you will be,
sowing your seed by every stream,
and letting your cattle and donkeys range free.
Isaiah 32:16-20

The Blessing of Righteousness is Peace

Isaiah describes the perfect life. Wouldn't you love to have a Christmas full of peace, quiet, and rest, and a secure and undisturbed place to live?

Like most of Isaiah's prophecies, these verses have a double message. This time, the first is a word of hope for Israel, something to help them through the exile; the second is an event that will happen much later, maybe at the end of history.

Israel looked forward to a time of peace—a day when enemy attacks would cease, and they could rebuild war torn homes. The Almighty promised them the blessing they longed for.

Isaiah proclaimed this two-fold promise for us, too. When we live in our Savior's goodness and justice, we receive the blessing of peace and rest, an unexplainable calm. Even when bad things happen, like hail flattening a forest, the people who live under Christ's righteousness remain blessed.

This blessing of peace was born at Christmas. It's only available because God came to earth as a Baby in a manger. Jesus entered our world to show us how much He cares and demonstrate a life worth living. He lived to be our righteousness.

And more than that, because advent includes looking forward to Christ's coming again, we also read these words from Isaiah as a blessing for the future. One day the people of God will know complete peace. Better than peace in the midst of hard times, when Christ comes again, we will be completely free of life's difficulties, and heavenly peace will be more than words in a blessing.

The Second Saturday of Advent
The Candle of Blessing

*"The Lord bless you
and keep you;
the Lord make his face shine on you
and be gracious to you;
the Lord turn his face toward you
and give you peace."
So [the priests] will put my name on the Israelites,
and I will bless them.*
Numbers 6:24-27

An Ancient Blessing of Peace

As we come to the end of our second week of advent, we'll share what may be the oldest blessing of peace in human history. When Moses shared God's expectations with His chosen people, He gave these words to Aaron and his descendants. God asked the priests to repeatedly speak this blessing over God's people, and by doing so, put the Name of the Lord on them so they could be blessed.

We now have less than two weeks to find gifts for those we love most. What if this year we could give them the perfect gift?

Few gifts truly "keep on giving," as the old saying goes,

but this priestly blessing may fit the bill. Wouldn't it be a beautiful gift to pray these words over your family and friends?

> "May the Lord bless you and keep you;
> The Lord make His face to shine upon you,
> and be gracious to you.
> May the Lord turn His face towards you
> and grant you His peace."

May you be blessed with peace this advent, this Christmas, and always!

The Third Week of Advent

The Candle of Salvation

*If you're lighting candles,
this week you'll light three each evening.*

The Third Sunday of Advent
The Candle of Salvation

"'So do not be afraid, Jacob my servant;
do not be dismayed, Israel,'
declares the Lord.
'I will surely save you out of a distant place,
your descendants from the land of their exile.
Jacob will again have peace and security,
and no one will make him afraid.
Jeremiah 30:10

Salvation & Peace for God's Chosen

It's no secret that Jacob and his descendants, better known as Israel, are God's chosen. Unfortunately, they left their chosen status behind and followed other gods. As a result, they found themselves exiled nine hundred miles from home. As prisoners in a foreign land, they felt abandoned by God.

Israel's exile mirrors the repetitious story of humanity. Created in the image of the Father and living in perfection, humans give it all up when they don't trust the One who made them. Our sin separates us from Him. Like the people of Israel, we find ourselves feeling isolated in an emotional or spiritual sense.

Fortunately, Jesus' birth makes these verses a promise for us, too. When we make Bethlehem's Baby our Savior, we inherit Jeremiah's blessing. God wants to save his people, Israel, as well as the followers of Jesus Christ, from "distant places."

God wants us back in that perfect relationship. Jesus came to restore us. He traded His place in heaven for a life of poverty and a painful death so His Spirit could give us peace and security. This week enjoy the salvation Jesus came to bring and embrace His peace as God's chosen people.

The Third Monday of Advent
The Candle of Salvation

Therefore, since we have been justified through faith,
we have peace with God
through our Lord Jesus Christ
Romans 5:1

Salvation by Faith Brings Peace

All around the world the population looks for peace, and even more during this season. Somewhere deep inside every person rests an awareness that peace is attainable. God created a place in each soul that longs for and believes in the possibility of peace on earth. Christmas songs promise this tranquility, but many look for it in the gifts and the season instead of the One who was born to bring it.

Paul encapsulates the promise of peace perfectly in these few words from his letter to the Christians in Rome: "Since we have been justified [given salvation] through faith, we have peace …"

A rich man once asked Jesus, "What can I do for salvation?" This young man knew that the peace he longed for came packaged with salvation. He searched for the fruit; but missed it because he wasn't willing to give up the things that stole his peace.

Two thousand years later, people everywhere search for peace just as diligently as that wealthy young adult. They look for help in books and material possessions, from therapists and friends. Some even search in churches or synagogues, and while there is value in all these things, none can bring true, complete peace.

Paul said, "Since we have been justified through faith …" Salvation comes through faith, faith that God keeps His promises, faith that those who follow Christ are God's chosen people, faith that a Baby in a manger grew to be a sacrifice for our sins. And not only does He give life everlasting in heaven; He can also grant life abundant here on earth.

A problem arises when we seek peace before salvation, because Paul clearly tells us salvation through faith in Jesus Christ opens the gates to true and everlasting peace. So, as you light a few candles or simply say a prayer in these last days of advent, seek the salvation that Christ came to give. Because when you do, you will also find peace.

The Third Tuesday of Advent
The Candle of Salvation

If you follow my decrees
and are careful to obey my commands,
I will send you rain in its season,
and the ground will yield its crops and the trees their fruit.
Your threshing will continue until grape harvest
and the grape harvest will continue until planting,
and you will eat all the food you want
and live in safety in your land.
I will grant peace in the land,
and you will lie down and no one will make you afraid.
. . .
I will look on you with favor . . .
and I will keep my covenant with you.
. . .
I will put my dwelling place among you,
and I will not abhor you.
I will walk among you and be your God,
and you will be my people.
I am the Lord your God . . .
I broke the bars of your yoke
and enabled you to walk with heads held high.
Leviticus 26:3-13

Salvation, Peace & Prosperity

What a promise! Thousands of years before Christ visited Earth, our heavenly Father created a covenant with His chosen people. God promised to provide and protect anyone who would obey His commands and follow His word. And the beauty of this covenant lies in the fact that those who trust the Baby in the manger for their salvation are the people of God's favor.

It's hard work making sure we follow every command and decree the Almighty has ever spoken, but Jesus said He came to fulfill the Law! (Matthew 5:17) So when we love and follow Him with all our heart, soul, and mind, the Son of God becomes our righteousness. This promise from Leviticus becomes ours!

Millennia before that peaceful night in Bethlehem, God told His people that He would put His "dwelling place among" them. How could they have known Yahweh meant His Spirit would live in the hearts of His people? And when the Creator said He would one day "walk among us," they had no idea a Baby would be born to fulfill this promise.

I'm sure the people of Moses' time never imagined the Creator would make His home in a stable so He could break the yoke of sin and grant salvation. But God kept His promise, because with Jesus we can hold our heads high as He pours out His perfect peace.

The Third Wednesday of Advent
The Candle of Salvation

The Lord swore an oath to David,
a sure oath he will not revoke:
"One of your own descendants
I will place on your throne.
If your sons keep my covenant
and the statutes I teach them,
then their sons will sit
on your throne for ever and ever."
For the Lord has chosen Zion,
he has desired it for his dwelling, saying,
"This is my resting place for ever and ever;
here I will sit enthroned, for I have desired it.
I will bless her with abundant provisions;
her poor I will satisfy with food.
I will clothe her priests with salvation,
and her faithful people will ever sing for joy.
"Here I will make a horn grow for David
and set up a lamp for my anointed one.
I will clothe his enemies with shame,
but his head will be adorned with a radiant crown."
Psalm 132:11-18

God's Chosen Clothed with Salvation and Peace

Though the Old Testament never reveals the precise identity of the Messiah, hints and foreshadows can be found in nearly every book. These few verses from Psalm 132 give us a perfect example.

Matthew and Luke both trace Jesus' lineage to King David. He is the descendant destined to sit on the throne forever. Now that the Savior has returned to heaven, he wears that radiant crown. But the best part of this prophecy comes in verse sixteen. It's a promise of salvation for the priests, and as we said in the first week of Advent, according to 1 Peter 2:9, you and I are a part of a royal priesthood.

The Psalm also makes a promise to Zion, better known as Jerusalem. The chosen city would be God's resting place. But as in many prophecies, there is second Zion, another place chosen by God for His dwelling: YOU. Christ's coming, death, and resurrection, opened the way for God's Spirit to rest in our hearts and minds. Jesus' birth created the opportunity for the faithful to be priests.

If Christ is your Savior, then you, my friend, are God's resting place, His dwelling of peace. His Spirit is within you, and you are the priest that He has clothed with salvation. You are His faithful people singing for joy!

The Third Thursday of Advent
The Candle of Salvation

Therefore this is what the Sovereign Lord says to them:
See, I myself will judge
between the fat sheep and the lean sheep.
Because you shove with flank and shoulder,
butting all the weak sheep with your horns
until you have driven them away,
I will save my flock, and they will no longer be plundered.
I will judge between one sheep and another.
I will place over them one shepherd, my servant David,
and he will tend them;
he will tend them and be their shepherd.
I the Lord will be their God,
and my servant David will be prince among them.
I the Lord have spoken.
I will make a covenant of peace with them
. . .
You are my sheep, the sheep of my pasture,
and I am your God,
declares the Sovereign Lord.
Ezekiel 34:20-25a & 31

Salvation that Brings Peace

In every generation people have used their physical or political power to intimidate and shove others around. Bullies existed in Ezekiel's day, too. But after reading today's verses, I think tyrants should think twice before tormenting God's chosen.

The Father promises salvation to His chosen. His sheep received an everlasting covenant: the Prince would one day live among them. Hundreds of years before the star appeared to the wise men, Ezekiel prophesied the coming of a Shepherd from the family of King David—a Shepherd to take care of those bullies, a Caretaker to bring peace

Though Ezekiel's words speak of a time in the future, these verses become relevant today for the person who chooses to live in the protective shadow of the Almighty's personal Shepherd.

Ezekiel knew salvation would come for God's people. He believed Yahweh would send a Shepherd to walk among humans and pour out showers of blessings. Ezekiel understood that this Savior would protect the chosen from being devoured; His sheep no longer need to live in fear. The prophet didn't realize that the name of the Shepherd, the One who would bring ultimate salvation and peace, would be Jesus.

The Third Friday of Advent
The Candle of Salvation

He had no beauty or majesty to attract us to him,
nothing in his appearance that we should desire him.
He was despised and rejected by mankind,
a man of suffering, and familiar with pain.
Like one from whom people hide their faces
he was despised, and we held him in low esteem.

. . .

But he was pierced for our transgressions,
he was crushed for our iniquities;
the punishment that brought us peace was on him,
and by his wounds we are healed.
We all, like sheep, have gone astray,
each of us has turned to our own way;
and the Lord has laid on him the iniquity of us all.
He was oppressed and afflicted, yet he did not open his mouth;
he was led like a lamb to the slaughter,
and as a sheep before its shearers is silent,
so he did not open his mouth.

. . .

For he was cut off from the land of the living;
for the transgression of my people he was punished.

. . .

Yet it was the Lord's will to crush him and cause him to suffer, and though the Lord makes his life an offering for sin,

. . .

After he has suffered,
he will see the light of life and be satisfied;
by his knowledge my righteous servant will justify many,
and he will bear their iniquities.

. . .

because he poured out his life unto death,
Isaiah 53

His Punishment: Our Salvation & Peace

During advent, we like to focus on the manger and the star, the wise men and shepherds, and the angels bringing good news on a peaceful night. We prefer to save this piece of prophecy from Isaiah for Good Friday.

As we prepare for Christmas, it's much more pleasant to memorialize Jesus as the Light of life, God's righteous Servant, the tender shoot, and precious Baby, who, as "Away in the Manger" would have us believe, never cried, as laughable as that may be.

But when we discuss salvation that brings peace, it's imperative we remember that God always knew the baby would be despised and rejected. Mary's Son came to suffer and take up our pain. He walked on this earth to be pierced for our transgressions; all our wrongs crushed Him. Jesus lived to die, and the punishment He received, the wounds He endured, brings our healing and provides true peace.

The Third Saturday of Advent
The Candle of Salvation

When one of the Pharisees invited Jesus
to have dinner with him,
he went to the Pharisee's house and reclined at the table.
A woman in that town who lived a sinful life
learned that Jesus was eating at the Pharisee's house,
so she came there with an alabaster jar of perfume.
As she stood behind him at his feet weeping,
she began to wet his feet with her tears.
Then she wiped them with her hair,
kissed them and poured perfume on them.

. . .

Therefore, I tell you, [Simon]
her many sins have been forgiven—
as her great love has shown.
But whoever has been forgiven little loves little."
Then Jesus said to her, "Your sins are forgiven."
The other guests began to say among themselves,
"Who is this who even forgives sins?"
Jesus said to the woman,
"Your faith has saved you; go in peace."
Luke 7:36-50

Faith brings Salvation, Salvation brings Peace

A woman with a bad reputation comes to Jesus. Her weeping demonstrates she understands her sin has separated her from her true Father, and somehow, even before Jesus' death, she inherently knows that this man can restore that estranged relationship. She has so much gratitude and faith she makes a spectacle of herself. The gift she brought costs more than she can afford to give, and she seems to have little expectation of anything in return.

This sinful woman's attitude gives us a perfect picture of the true Spirit of Christmas.

We have been separated from our loving Father by generations of lies, doubt, and mistrust. Like this woman, we have done things that have broken our relationship with the One who loves us more than we can possibly imagine. We long for peace. We want to personally know God's perfect love; yet fear and pride hold us back. Hesitant to give Jesus more than we can afford, we're embarrassed to love him recklessly in front of others who might ridicule.

As we end this week of considering the Salvation and Peace that Christ came to give to God's chosen, think for a moment about the gifts you'll be giving this season. Some you'll give out of obligation, but most you'll deliver with love. What kind of gift do you plan to give to Jesus? Will it show your love and devotion or your fear of what people think? Will it be a gift of reckless abandon or a token of duty? Most important to consider—will it be a gift of faith? Will it inspire Jesus to say, "Your faith has saved you; go in peace"?

The Fourth Week of Advent

The Candle of Tranquility

*If you're lighting candles,
this week you'll light four each evening.*

*We are about to enter the fourth week of Advent.
Depending on the year,
you may not need all of the readings for this week.
Just keep reading through
until Christmas Eve.
On December 24, simply turn
to the last reading in the book.*

The Fourth Sunday of Advent
The Candle of Tranquility

Let them come to me for refuge;
let them make peace with me,
yes, let them make peace with me.
Isaiah 27:5

Tranquility and Refuge in my Creator

Tranquility—what a beautiful word. It brings visions of sunny places and quiet streams. This time of year, you might picture a snow-covered field on a starry night. People constantly look for tranquil moments in the chaos of life.

As the countdown to Christmas moves into the single digits, much of the world scurries around feeling anything but peace and tranquility.

Isn't it strange how we allow our celebration of the Prince of Peace to rob us of the tranquility God wants to give? We look for repose in carols, lights, and church services. But our heavenly Father tells us to come to Him for refuge. During these final days of advent, come to God—rest in His love. Take some time to forget about your to-do list and enjoy some tranquility in the Baby born to be your Peace.

The Fourth Monday of Advent
The Candle of Tranquility

Do not be anxious about anything, but in every situation,
by prayer and petition, with thanksgiving,
present your requests to God.
And the peace of God,
which transcends all understanding,
will guard your hearts and your minds
in Christ Jesus.
Philippians 4:6-7

Tranquility Beyond Understanding

These verses have the potential to be the best gift you receive this Christmas. Pray about everything and trust in the Baby in the manger. Then the peace only God can give, a tranquility that goes beyond human understanding, will protect and keep us.

It seems like a simple task, yet most of us make it quite difficult. We trust our jobs, put hope in our bank accounts, and lean on our friends. God tells us not to be anxious, but we worry about everything.

Tonight, as you pray, tell God your worries. Every time you catch yourself overthinking, give it to Jesus. As we train ourselves to trust Him, each new concern will be easier to release.

Christ has everything under control. Be thankful for Jesus Christ, His birth, His death, His resurrection, and His mighty love. Pray about every situation, and Christ will fill you with peace, not just at Christmas, but always.

The Fourth Tuesday of Advent
The Candle of Tranquility

Answer me when I call to you,
my righteous God.
Give me relief from my distress;
have mercy on me and hear my prayer.

. . .

In peace I will lie down and sleep,
for you alone, Lord,
make me dwell in safety.
Psalm 4:1 & 8

Peace and Tranquility when I Sleep

When was the last time you got a good night's sleep? Do you toss and turn, anxious about everything you didn't get done today? During this busy time, our to-do lists grow longer than usual, and we often stay up late trying to check off as many things as possible.

But David, the man after God's heart and Jesus' most famous ancestor, knew what to do. He cried out to His Creator, then trusted God. With His Heavenly Father in charge, David didn't give the matter a second thought. He went to bed free from anxiety, free from harm.

I believe that's why Joseph Mohr's last minute candlelight service creation is one of the world's favorite

Christmas carols. Besides its beautiful melody and simple lyrics, "Silent Night" reminds us that our Savior's perfect nature and His ability to trust in His Father even from birth would have allowed Him to "Sleep in Heavenly Peace" even as an infant.

As you prepare to sleep in these final days before Christmas, don't let the preparations, the buying, wrapping, baking, and more overtake the gift God wants to give you. Take some time to listen for His voice and experience the perfect tranquility of His heavenly peace.

The Fourth Wednesday of Advent
The Candle of Tranquility

All this I have spoken while still with you.
But the Advocate, the Holy Spirit, whom the Father
will send in my name, will teach you all things
and will remind you of everything I have said to you.
Peace I leave with you; my peace I give you.
I do not give to you as the world gives.
Do not let your hearts be troubled and do not be afraid.
You heard me say, 'I am going away
and I am coming back to you.'
If you loved me, you would be glad
that I am going to the Father, for the Father is greater than I.
I have told you now before it happens,
so that when it does happen you will believe.
I will not say much more to you,
for the prince of this world is coming.
He has no hold over me,
but he comes so that the world may learn
that I love the Father
and do exactly what my Father has commanded me.
John 14:25-31

Peace and Tranquility until the Second Advent

Our celebration of the first advent of Jesus Christ will be here soon, and in the midst of the hustle and bustle, we'd like to have some peace. In fact, even if you're alone for the holiday, without all the unrest brought on by a big celebration, you might still be looking for peace in lieu of loneliness.

Hours before Jesus faced the cross, He promised peace—not the world's style of peace, but true tranquility. Our Savior promised an unexplainable stillness deep within, rest that can only be found when His Spirit permeates our heart and soul.

If peace continues to elude you this season, I encourage you to read the entire fourteenth chapter of John. Jesus went straight from predicting Peter's denial to reassuring us we don't need to stress! Then He promised we could have anything we ask for in His name.

John 14 records Jesus' promise to never leave us. Our Savior wants us to have the gift of the Holy Spirit, and although He'll give this gift anytime of the year, wouldn't Christmas be a great time to ask Him for it?

If you find yourself still searching for the peace Jesus promised to give, perhaps you've never asked His Holy Spirit to rule in your life. When we let Christ's Spirit in, He sends Himself to keep our hearts from being troubled. The fullness of the Counselor helps us have no fear.

This Christmas unwrap Jesus' most sought-after gift. His gift of Salvation is the most precious, but His gift of the Holy Spirit is His most powerful, and it's this gift that allows us to experience the thing most treasured, true tranquility, perfect peace.

The Fourth Thursday of Advent
The Candle of Tranquility

Those who live according to the flesh
have their minds set on what the flesh desires;
but those who live in accordance with the Spirit
have their minds set on what the Spirit desires.
The mind governed by the flesh is death,
but the mind governed by the Spirit is life and peace.
Romans 8:6

Life and Tranquility From the Spirit

Jesus wants to give you peace. Hopefully, you've begun to embrace that theme for yourself in the last twenty-five days. Jesus willingly gave up His spot at the right hand of the Father for a time so He could be born in the humblest of circumstances. He left perfection just for you, to restore your relationship with your Heavenly Father and to offer you peace.

I call the Spirit of Christ my gyroscope. A gyroscope is a spinning wheel inside a wheel, originally used to keep a ship from tossing and turning when the storms got bad. Wikipedia says gyroscopes keep ships "nearly fixed, regardless of the ... motion." We celebrate Christmas because Jesus came to be your salvation and your gyroscope.

Okay, perhaps you don't call Him your gyroscope. But regardless, when we allow the Holy Spirit to be in charge, we can experience peace.

As Christmas looms closer, be sure you have allowed the Spirit of Christ to lead you in all that you do. Because when we do, we receive the greatest gifts of all, the gifts of life and peace.

The Fourth Friday of Advent
The Candle of Tranquility

May the God of hope
fill you with all joy and peace
as you trust in him,
so that you may overflow with hope
by the power of the Holy Spirit.
Romans 15:13

Benediction of Peace and Tranquility

We started advent with promises and blessings, and I'd like to finish the season on the same note. These words from Paul are a benediction, a blessing usually found at the end of a service or a letter. And this benediction holds my wish for you this season.

I see people everywhere searching for these Spirit-given gifts, they think hope, joy, and peace can be found in the perfect present or party. Some search in a child's face and many will attend church tomorrow night, not to worship the One born to die, but in search of peace.

So many folks experience difficulty finding these gifts, but they are not hidden or even veiled in trappings like the presents under our tree. The Spirit's gifts are free for the taking, and with them come even more abundance and blessing than we can describe or imagine.

They are free because Jesus paid the price. He was born for us, He lived for us, He died for us, and He rose for us! He has done everything necessary so we can have these gifts; it's up to us to receive and open them. But many are afraid, because like every gift, they come with a bit of responsibility attached.

The gift of an expensive vase requires a safe shelf and a polishing cloth. The gift of a costly toy necessitates care so it doesn't get dropped or broken. And the gifts of salvation and peace require loving the One who offers the gift with our heart, soul, mind, and strength.

My friend, I wish you all the joy and peace Christ wants to give. I pray you will offer Christ your whole self, relinquishing control to His Spirit, so you might be filled with every ounce of the gifts the God of hope possesses. May you receive an abundance of the Spirit, and even more of His fruit, especially the fruit of heavenly peace.

Christmas Eve
The Candle of Christ

Luke 2:1-20

The Beginning of Heavenly Peace

It's here! The day we've been waiting for has arrived. But how has it come in your life? Has the advent of Christmas been full of turmoil or overflowing with peace?

After traveling nearly one hundred miles, over the length of a week or more, on the brink of delivering a baby, Mary's life might have been less than peaceful. Add to that the disappointment of not finding an available bed and ending up in animal housing instead; the couple probably felt a bit anxious.

However, almost every parent will confess: something unexplainable happens at the birth of your first child. As anxious and stressful as the hours leading up to the birth might be, the moments after become almost magical, and, except in extreme cases, peaceful.

By the time the shepherds showed up, Mary was already treasuring and pondering. No gifts had been opened; the Wise Men didn't come for months. The Baby's birth didn't bring a promise of prosperity or even a room for the night. But something about that Baby, maybe more than most, brought peace and the opportunity to savor every moment. Scripture tells us, Mary treasured each one in her heart.

This Christmas I pray we won't treasure the gifts or the wrappings. I hope we'll ignore the decorations and the meal. Instead, let's plan to appreciate the goodness of Christ, the beauty of His sacrifice, the majesty of His Father, and the power of His Spirit. I want to ponder His promises, bestow His blessings, savor his salvation, and treasure His tranquility as I learn to allow His Spirit to lead me and help me live in his perfect heavenly peace.

More by Lynne Modranski

Children's Curriculum

Jesus, Teach Me How to Pray
Heroes, Heroines, Champs and Chumps
The Fruit of the Spirit is . . .
The Bible Meets Potato Chip Science
Children of the King

Bible Studies

Dive In: To a Life of Freedom
I Really Want to Worship You, Lord
A Future and a Hope
40 Days in the Wilderness
Running the Race
Hope in Our Suffering

Devotion Books

More than Conquerors
First Steps for New Christians
Devotions Inspired by Life
Devotions for Church Leaders and Small Groups
A Reflection of the Beauty of God
Quiet Times for Busy Mom

About the Author

Lynne Modranski is an author, inspirational speaker, and Biblical coach who empowers Christian leaders and inspires spiritual growth; helping people move from rules to relationship and dive into Christ's abundance.

Wife to Steve, a local church pastor, she is mom to Monica, Sylvia, and Julia and "Hada" to Joshua, Corryn, Elizabeth, and Jaycee. Worship Leader and Small Groups Coordinator of Sycamore Tree Church, Lynne is first and foremost a follower of Jesus Christ. She has a passion to help others find a real relationship with the One who has given her true life as she shows them how they can become the very best they can be in Christ Jesus!

Lynne has written several Bible Studies, e-books, devotional readings, children's curricula, plays, and advent readings. Visit her website to find out more about her spiritual growth classes and one-on-one Biblical coaching.

Made in the USA
Las Vegas, NV
26 November 2023